A GENTLE
INTRODUCTION TO
BEATING
PROCRASTINATION
AND GETTING
FOCUSED

STEPHEN HAUNTS

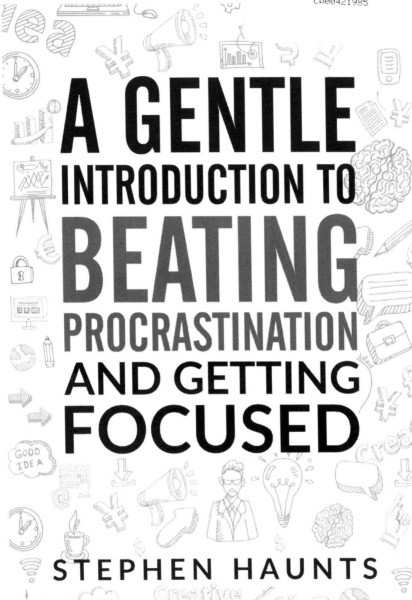

A Gentle Introduction to Beating Procrastination and Getting Focused

Identifying and Beating Procrastination to Better Focus on Your Work

A Gentle Introduction to Beating Procrastination and Getting Focused

by Stephen Haunts

Published by Stephen Haunts Ltd

www.stephenhaunts.com

© 2018 Stephen Haunts

Cover by Zeljka Kojic

Contents

This book is dedicated to my wife Amanda and my kids, Amy and Daniel, who are always putting up with my personal projects.

Thank you for purchasing, A Gentle Introduction to Beating Procrastination and Getting Focused. If you like this book, I would be very grateful for you leaving a review on Amazon. I read all reviews and will try to address any constructive feedback with updates to the book. You can review the book in your country at the following links, or from your local Amazon website.

Amazon.com
Amazon.co.uk
Amazon.de
Amazon.fr

If you enjoyed this book, you might like other books I have in the "Gentle Introduction To" series. I have written these short guides to focus on specific niches and make them brief enough to read in a short space of time, but also detailed enough that they offer a lot of value.

If you wish to see what other high-value books I have in this series, then please visit my web page at the following link.

Gentle Introduction To Book Series

About the Author

Stephen Haunts has been developing software and applications professionally since 1996 and as a hobby since he was 10. Stephen has worked in many different industries including computer games, online banking, retail finance, healthcare, and pharmaceuticals. Stephen started out programming in BASIC on machines such as the Dragon 32, Vic 20 and the Amiga and moved onto C and C++ on the IBM PC. Stephen has been developing software in C# and the .NET framework since first being introduced to it in 2003.

As well as being an accomplished software developer, Stephen is also an experienced development leader and has led, mentored and coached teams to deliver many high-value, high-impact solutions in finance and healthcare.

Outside of Stephen's day job, he is also an experienced tech blogger who runs a popular blog called Coding in the Trenches at www.stephenhaunts.com, and he is also a training course author for the popular online training company Pluralsight. Stephen also runs several open source projects including SafePad, Text Shredder, Block Encrpytor, and Smoke Tester—the post deployment testing tool.

Stephen is also an accomplished electronic musician and sound designer.

Introduction

Have you ever decided not to work on your important tasks and do some more trivial ones instead? If this is the case, then you are reading the right book.

Procrastination is one of the most common hindrances to productivity in the workplace and school. The performance of an excellent student or employee suffers when he or she starts to procrastinate. More than 80% of students and employees procrastinate in their work at some point. 20% of these except that they are chronic procrastinators.

This book will talk about how procrastination happens. It talks about how the habit can creep up into your routine and how even the most diligent student or employee can sometimes become a chronic procrastinator if they start to let go of their self-control.

In this book, we'll also talk about how you can change your mindset and your values so that you can get rid of this nasty habit. The process of beating procrastination all starts in mind. This book doesn't only talk about how you can gain control of your thoughts, but it also discusses how you can use habit building techniques to change your behavior towards difficult tasks.

Ultimately, your journey in beating procrastination will depend on how well you improve your focusing skills. To avoid procrastination in the future, you will need to learn how to focus on the tasks that you want to achieve.

Focus is not just about putting your mind into one thing or task. It involves a much wider scope. It starts with the way you choose your goals and your priorities. It is also connected to how you control your thoughts, not only during your workdays but also when you are resting.

This book will give you all this information in the hopes that it will lead you to become more productive at work or school. By investing your time in this book, you will have access to the best strategies on how to beat procrastination and gain the ability to focus. With these skills, you will create a mindset of doing high-quality work. Start reading this book today to start developing these skills.

Why I Wrote This Book?

Before you start reading this book, I first want to introduce myself and explain why I have written this book. My name is Stephen Haunts, and I am a software developer, trainer, writer and public speaker. I always felt that I had achieved a lot in my professional career, but earlier on, I had a big problem. That problem was that I was not very good at finishing something once I had started it.

For as long as I can remember I have always been the type of person that has liked to have personal projects outside of my full-time career. I would get excited about a project, do lots of initial work on it, but then my interest would falter, and when I was supposed to be working on that project I would start browsing the web, reading emails, watching videos, or anything except doing what I was supposed to be doing. I would event invent tasks to do, which I pretended were important, so I had a sense of achievement, yet they were not getting me to my actual goal. Eventually, I would get bored of that project and move on to something more exciting. I was a chronic procrastinator.

This would even become a running joke with my wife in that I never seemed to finish anything that I started. I decided that being someone who was so bad at completing projects was not acceptable; I needed to change my behaviors forever. Since then, I have built up some robust planning, concentration and focusing skills that allow me to complete any project I start with a good level of focus.

One of the things, I do now is write online training courses for a company called Pluralsight in the US. At the time of writing this book, I have published 13 of these courses, written five books, written and delivered many talks around the world at conferences and written and delivered multi-day training programs. All of this would have been impossible for me had I not taken a good long look at my working practices and made a conscious effort to change my behavior.

I have mentored many people to help them focus better on their work, and I decided to write this short book to help you too. I have tried to keep the length of this book as short as possible, while still delivering lots of information to help you. Let's face it; if you are reading this book, then you probably have a procrastination issue that you want to address, so a 300-page self-help book might not be the best idea.

If you find this book useful, then I would be very grateful if you could leave a rating and review over at Amazon. Reviews help me a lot and server as great feedback to help me improve my books.

Thanks, and I hope you enjoy this book. Your path to better focus and being procrastination free starts here.

Chapter 1 – What Is Procrastination?

We all experience procrastination on our tasks. It usually starts in school and brought to the workplace, when we are older, if not corrected. Many experts argue that the mind is just hardwired to procrastinate and that no one is exempted from this habit. Everyone needs to actively fight off this habit if they want to prevent the mediocre quality of work.

The first step in trying to beat procrastination is to try and understand it. With today's generation of managers who are so obsessed with productivity, we have gained a lot of information about procrastination and focus. Managers in both the public and private sectors all try to understand why their workers procrastinate. Let's start by discussing what is procrastination.

What is Procrastination?

Procrastination can be defined as the habit of putting tasks off. For some, it could be a habit of not working on important and challenging tasks. Some procrastinators just avoid these types of tasks until the deadline for the task is near.

Others also make themselves feel productive while procrastinating. They do this by choosing to do less urgent tasks instead of the tasks that they should be doing. This is commonly referred to as procrastiworking; appearing to work and be busy but working on the wrong tasks deliberately.

Procrastinators do not start doing scheduled tasks until they have no other choice but to do it. For students, for example, they usually procrastinate by delaying and doing their homework or take-home projects. Instead of doing their homework days before the deadline, they choose to do it on the day when they are supposed to submit it. Many students also procrastinate in their studies. Instead of studying every night to lighten the load, they choose to study and cram in the information only on the night before a big exam.

Procrastination in school often leads to the same behavior in the workplace. When a person procrastinates in the workplace, their chances for promotions are usually affected. An employee with a report due on Monday may wait until Monday morning to do it, before going to work.

Procrastinators are often good at getting out of the mess they've got themselves into in the first place. They keep procrastinating because they know that they can survive even with this habit.

The Dangers of Procrastinating

Procrastinating is one of the standard reasons why many people do not progress in life. They settle for giving only mediocre and even substandard effort to their work. With this mentality, they can often be the last people considered when promotions come.

Procrastination also affects your ability to reach your dreams and goals. We all have different ideas; some of us want to apply for a better paying job in a great company. We tell ourselves that we will update our resume and schedule an interview. Instead of pulling the trigger and getting the work done, we make up different excuses for rescheduling it.

Others want to start their own business. However, they tell themselves different reasons to justify why it is not the right time to do so. Some tell themselves that they do not have enough capital yet or that they do not have enough experience to do it. However, they do not do anything to come up with the money or to gain more experience.

They put off these tasks and do other tasks that are within their comfort zone. This is just another form of procrastination. Instead of working on their dreams, they keep on working on the job they hate because it is familiar, less stressful, and easy.

These are just some examples of dreams that are derailed by procrastination. I am sure that you have your dream or goal that you are putting off right now. Because these types of tasks do not come with deadlines, procrastinators do not have an external motivator to work on these types of tasks. If nothing changes, the procrastinator will never attain his dream.

Aside from this, procrastinators also experience higher instances of work-related stress than non-procrastinators. Because procrastinators are constantly chasing after deadlines, they are usually placed into tense working situations. This additional stress not only clutters the mind and affects their quality of work; prolonged exposure to it can also create health problems. Higher stress levels at work are related to heart conditions, depression, substance abuse (drugs or alcohol) and other types of negative health conditions.

In contrast, beating procrastination does not only releases you from constant workplace-related stress, but it also clears your mind of clutter. The more you procrastinate, the longer the thoughts of work stay in your mind. Thoughts of your unfinished work will keep on coming back until you finish it. Your mind will bear less stress if you could clear it of unnecessary thoughts about your unfinished work.

Working on challenging tasks ahead of time also gives you the ability to become competitive when you are aiming for promotions or better job offers. Procrastinators often develop a negative reputation in the workplace.

A person with this kind of habit is often identified to have poor work ethics. People hate working with procrastinators because their quality of work is usually negatively affected by the procrastinator's disregard of best practices in identifying priorities and time management. As a result, a group that depends on the work of a procrastinator often ends up creating inferior quality products.

Now that we understand how procrastination affects our ability to perform in school and the workplace let's discuss why we procrastinate.

Why Do We Procrastinate?

Everyone has their reasons for procrastinating. Most people never learn why they tend to procrastinate. Because of this, they never get to the root of their bad work habit. If you wish to get rid of it, you should learn why you choose to put off your tasks and why you tend to avoid work that you deem difficult.

Check the following reasons behind procrastination and see if you can relate your situation to it.

Fear of Failure

The procrastinator tries to avoid challenging tasks because they are afraid of failing. They often overthink what the task requires. This is the reason why they tell themselves that they need more 'preparation' before they could start working. This so-called preparation though ends up being just another method they use so that they can avoid the tasks that they consider unpleasant.

Much of the reasons behind their fear of failure stem from social factors. Many procrastinators fear failure because they worry what other people may say about their work. Some are afraid of being ridiculed when they fail while others fear to disappoint the people they look up to.

To overcome this type of procrastination, you should reflect on your fear of failure and how your relationships are with the people around you. It is important to remember that you still need to work on the things that you put off. This means that by procrastinating, you are not getting rid of the problem. Instead, you are only delaying your progress.

It is also essential for you to remember that no one will rescue you when you procrastinate. The people around you will not be able to help you. You will eventually need to face these tasks yourself; delaying the inevitable only prolongs the burden.

In most cases, a procrastinator's social fear does not have a basis. The people around you may not pay attention to whether you succeed or not. You should not care about what other people say or think. This way, you will not be intimidated by your tasks, and you will be able to start working on them when it is time to do so.

I will admit that this fear of failure used to be my biggest concern, which is why I have listed it first. Over the years, I have trained myself not to worry or care about other people's opinions of me or my work. This takes time to condition yourself mentally, but once you achieve it, it is very liberating.

Procrastinating makes the problem worse. By delaying progress on your work, you are only increasing your chance of failure. You'll improve your chance of success just by working on your tasks.

Think of work as your ticket to success. If you do less of it, your chance of success also lessens. The more working effort you put into a task, the higher your chance of success.

Procrastinators are Perfectionists

Procrastinators can often be perfectionists. They do not want to start something unprepared, or they do not want to take on a task at the wrong time. They really want to do a perfect job. If they think that they cannot achieve perfection, they make this their reason for not working.

Some would tell themselves that they are not prepared to do it. Others would say that they first need to do some other tasks like making coffee or getting a snack before starting to work.

All these excuses happen because the procrastinator is worried that the task will not be done right when they start prematurely. This reflects not only in small tasks but also in big, life-changing ones.

This type of procrastinator has a picture in their mind of the perfect outcome. Any factor that may prevent them from reaching this outcome affects their enthusiasm about the task. A person applying for a job may tell themselves that they do not have the right clothes for the interview or that there is something wrong with the resume and cover letter printed. The true value of these seemingly small issues is amplified in the mind of the procrastinator. He uses these small issues to justify rescheduling the task.

This is a common behavior among all types of procrastinators. They wait until the so-called perfect moment to start working. Unfortunately, the perfect moment never actually arrives for most people. Many people who delay starting on their goals end up abandoning their dreams. They usually settle for mediocrity.

Again, I list this one near the beginning because this used to be me. I was a chronic perfectionist to the point of never starting anything. My wife even joked that I had all these great ideas but never followed through with them or completed anything.

Low Energy Levels

Procrastination can stem from physiological issues as well; it often happens because a person lacks sufficient nutrition. People with an unhealthy diet or irregular eating patterns often fall victim to this habit. This happens because they feel low on energy or hungry when they are supposed to be working. Instead of starting to work immediately, they procrastinate by looking for food or finding other reasons to avoid working.

Often, low energy levels do not necessarily mean that you need food. Many cases of lethargy are also attributed to dehydration. Lack of water in the body affects our ability to make the right decisions.

Lack of sleep can also lead to lethargy and the urge to procrastinate. The threat of procrastination is most active when our body is weak. When we lack sleep, our willpower weakens. Our mind's self-regulation functions fail us because the body and the brain prioritize resting and recuperating. The body is stressed when we lack sleep. It first wants to recover from this stressful state before our willpower to work increases again.

Our willpower is most potent right after waking up from a good night's sleep. When you have enough sleep, you are more likely to win the battle between resting and working. The body does not necessarily want to relax. Instead, the urge to work on one's goals becomes stronger than the urge to take a nap.

Lack of Focus

Your ability to concentrate is an essential factor in your fight against procrastination. Many procrastinators fail to put their mind on just one task at a time. People who have this problem are in danger of becoming overwhelmed by their workload.

This habit of stretching your energy and time too thinly can lead to exhaustion and lack of energy. Your energy levels may be depleted before you accomplish anything. If you are already tired before you achieve any of your goals, your motivation will begin to dwindle. Your hyped state of mind when you started is no longer there to fuel you to start working again. At this point, the influence of procrastination becomes even stronger.

Lack of focus can also happen when there are too many things trying to get your attention. With today's media-heavy environment, we have more stimulation around us taking our attention from our goals. Most people carry a smartphone or a tablet everywhere they go. These tools give us a wide range of entertainment choices. They also provide us with access to the internet which opens up to a lot more opportunities for distractions.

Many of us develop addictions to these devices and the apps in them without even realizing it. We end up missing the chance to start on essential tasks at the right time because of them.

Our constant reliance on these apps and devices for entertainment often affects our effectiveness in the workplace.

Whenever we feel stressed, we turn to them to make us feel good. This happens when we are required to do unpleasant tasks. The stress from these tasks often makes procrastination as an attractive alternative.

How Procrastination Happens

Procrastination happens because our brain tries to take shortcuts in its quest for happiness. Our mind is focused on keeping us alive. It does this by creating emotions to drive our actions. The brain produces positive emotions like happiness and contentment to encourage behavior that will improve our chances of survival. Behavior that leads to finding food is associated with the sensation of being full. This is partnered with happiness and the feeling of contentment.

In contrast, behaviors that lead to pain are treated with fear. Uncertainty may lead to danger and danger should be avoided at all times, if an organism is to survive. The same mechanism operates when we encounter a new and challenging task. When we see this type of task, the uncertainty prompts our brain to generate fear.

Fear, on the other hand, is a mechanism that leads to one of either two reactions, fight or flight. The first response is to fight against the source of the fear. When this reaction kicks in, the body gets ready to defend itself through aggression or confrontation.

In the ancient times, this response allowed our ancestors to fight off predators and rival tribes. This response is sometimes appropriate for our survival. It is usually used by the brain when it is desperate.

A caveman will only explore a cave when there is a good chance of finding food and other survival items. Otherwise, they will try to avoid this type of place because of the uncertainty of what may be inside. If it can be avoided, our brain does not want to use the fight response. Usually doing so means putting our bodies in risky situations.

The opposite of the fear response is to turn away from the cause of the fear and to run away from it. Behavioral psychologists refer to this type of behavior as the flight response. The flight response is the preferred course of action of the brain because it has lesser risk than the alternative.

In this response, the brain tells the body to carry out behaviors that limit risk and avoids confrontation. This is the best response to many of the real threats to our ancestor's life.

In the modern work and living environment, there are hardly any threats to our lives anymore. In the civilized world, we are taught to live in peace and avoid situations where our lives may be in danger. The authorities in our society treat peace and order as a priority.

Even with significantly fewer dangerous elements to deal with, our old fight and flight mechanism still exists to keep us out of harm's way. However, instead of being applied in survival situations, it is usually applied to our everyday tasks. The fear mechanism is triggered by anything new that may lead to an unpleasant feeling.

When we learn about a new task, the brain instantly creates fear of it because of the uncertainty that it brings. This triggers the fight or flight response to deal with the cause of the fear. The ideal response to beat procrastination is to fight or face the problem. In this situation, the fight response is to start doing the work.

As stated above, however, the brain prefers to avoid using the fight response if it can be helped. Many procrastinators started the habit of putting tasks off with this simple mechanism.

26

This habit usually starts in school. Most of the students put off tasks like studying, doing projects or homework. When they cram and submit a mediocre project, they are still given a passing grade. Nobody ever calls them out for not putting in the time to do their task.

This behavior is usually carried over to the workplace when procrastinator students enter the workforce. In the beginning, the new worker or employee may do everything by the book. As they learn the rules and practices in the new workplace, they also learn of the shortcuts in their work.

One of these shortcuts is procrastination. They learn the parts of the job that they can procrastinate on and the parts where they should not. Over time, this habit becomes stronger and is carried until the worker is promoted to higher positions. It all started with the fight and flight mechanism that we inherited from our ancestors.

Procrastination and Fear

Fear is a powerful tool that our brain uses to adjust our behaviors. In the previous section, we talked about how the subtle worries of everyday life lead us to procrastinate. The fear that leads us to procrastinate also motivates us to start working on our tasks when the deadline is near.

Our fear of the task is replaced by our fear of being punished for not doing the work. In the workplace, not doing the work may be punished with an earful or a sermon from a boss. At this point, the brain can no longer use the flight response to run away from the source of the fear. Instead, the brain shifts to the fight response. This behavior shift makes us do the necessary work and avoid the punishments that come with not working. For most people, most of the work is done within a few hours before the deadline. This behavioral pattern has become the usual routine for most procrastinators.

Shifting to the Proactive Mindset

Procrastinators usually develop a reactive approach when dealing with the sources of their fears. They allow the fear to establish in their minds and they enable their tendencies and old bad habits to dictate their response. To beat procrastination and to develop the ability to focus on your tasks, you will need to develop a proactive mindset.

When a person is proactive, they are always thinking of making things better for their future self. With this mindset, you are still looking into what you can do now so that your future self will not be in a dangerous situation. If you develop this mindset, you will no longer allow yourself to be reactive to fear. Proactive people already start working even before the fear kicks in.

To become proactive, you need to put all your tasks in their designated timeslots and follow through with your planning. By following through, we mean that you need to work when your schedule says so.

For people with a long-term of procrastination habits, this is easier said than done. In the following chapters, we will talk about how you can get over your fear and retarget your focus towards the more critical tasks.

Chapter 2 – The First Steps to Overcome Procrastination

Overcoming procrastination will be a lifelong process. The moment you let your guard down, procrastination will creep back into your day to day activities. In this chapter, we will lay the foundation for ending your procrastination habit. Let's start with the skill of self-awareness.

Awareness

The first step to overcoming procrastination is always to become more aware of your weaknesses. You need to learn what tasks you often procrastinate on and when you tend to procrastinate on them. You should also learn what your preferred method of procrastination is.

By learning about your behavior, you can find ways to anticipate procrastination. You can start being aware of keeping a work journal. In this journal, you should write about all the things that you worked on a particular day. Most office workers are already doing this. They create a report on what they did on a specific period and submit it to their bosses.

You can do the same. Instead of a progress report, you can aim to create a detailed list of the things that you did for a particular day. Do this task for a week until you have enough information to start on.

Keeping a personal diary or journal can be useful in keeping track of your thoughts. The more you work to get rid of procrastination, the more lessons you will learn along the way.

If you do not keep track of these experiences, you are likely to forget them.

People who struggle to deal with procrastination fall into cycles. They plan out strategies that help them stop procrastination. After a while, they become complacent, and they forget all the systems that they developed. As they start to become complacent, their old habit starts to creep back into their routines. They begin to procrastinate again.

A procrastination journal or diary helps in making you remember about your journey. You should try to continue keeping your anti-procrastination journal or diary even after you have succeeded in stopping procrastination. This way, you will be able to go back to your old thoughts and remind yourself of the journey you took to get rid of it.

Even if you find yourself procrastinating again, you no longer need to start from step one all over again. You just need to go back to your journal or diary and redo the best practices you have developed in the past.

By doing this, you start to paint a picture of your daily routine. Check your weeks' worth of data and analyze it. First, you need to start identifying the essential tasks in your day. Next, you need to determine the vital tasks that you tend to avoid. After that, think of why you tend to avoid them. Do you hate doing them because of the amount of thinking they require? Or do you hate the menial labor?

Try to find the right reasons behind why you tend to avoid the task. If you could accurately identify your reasons for doing so, you will be able to pick the right strategies for keeping your focus on the task.

Procrastination Outside of the Office

Getting rid of procrastination is not only a professional improvement project; by getting rid of this habit, you will be able to improve your effectiveness in all aspects of your life.

When we talk about procrastination, we often refer to the business or office setting. However, aside from that area of your life, there are many other areas in life where we tend to procrastinate. Some career-driven parents may tend to procrastinate their bonding time with their children. Some people procrastinate in their adult responsibilities like paying off debt or starting a retirement fund. Almost all of us procrastinate on working towards our dreams.

Most of us will procrastinate most of the things that are outside of our work area. If you want to improve holistically, you should remove procrastination in all aspects of your life.

Developing Your Drive for Self-Improvement

If you want to develop holistically in getting rid of procrastination, you need to motivate yourself to improve. To drive yourself to embark on this journey, you will need to go back to your roots. Explore your reasons for working and performing the type of tasks you do in your work. What are your goals for yourself and the people you love? Are your goals right now still those same goals that you created when you graduated in college?

By exploring our sources of motivation, we will be able to learn where we will be most happy. It is common for people who are not satisfied with their job to procrastinate. Because they hate the job, they tend to avoid putting too much time and thoughts into it.

You will need to explore your reasons for procrastinating if you want to improve. By learning these things, you will be able to create the best strategy against it. In this book, we talk about how you can get rid of procrastination in general. However, for some people, the tricks in this book may not be enough.

Someone who hates their job and constantly tries to delay their work, for example, is better off looking for a new job that will make them happier. If you are satisfied with what you are doing and if you believe that your position has an essential role in your life or society, you are less likely to procrastinate.

To keep your drive for self-improvement high, make sure that your goals and your daily activities are aligned with your happiness. If necessary, find a new job that is aligned with your personal goals. If your daily activity is not aligned with your goals, you are less likely to enjoy what you are doing. This mismatch increases the likelihood of procrastination.

Decreasing your chances of procrastination

Accepting That We Are Not Perfect

To convince yourself to work on the tasks that you have been putting off in the past, you will need to change your mindset. One of the principles that you need to tell yourself is that your tasks will never be perfect, nor does it need to be. There will always be factors that will prevent you from doing an excellent job.

It is also essential for you to remember that the tasks we do will only be done well if we give them enough time. The more time you put into a task, the better its product will be. You need to stop waiting for the perfect time to start your work. That "perfect" moment might never arrive.

Instead, work on the task as soon as possible. By giving a task more of your time, you will have more opportunities to check your output and to improve it. If mistakes are made or if some parts of your plan do not work out, you will still have enough time to correct them or to re-strategize them.

You can only do this if you start working on a task as early as possible. Your output will be close to perfect if you give yourself enough time to check and improve it.

Understand That Failure is not Fatal

You can also stop procrastinating by remembering that failure is just a regular part of the journey to success. Everyone will fail at some point in their lives. The more critical factor is how we react in the wake of these failures.

Think of it this way, the sooner you try out those ideas, the sooner you will learn if they will work or not. The more ideas you try out, the more chances you have to become successful in your task. You can only maximize the number of tries you get if you start as early as possible.

Failing is only a sign that there is something wrong with your plan or in its execution. It does not mean that there is something wrong with you. Most of our failures only have temporary effects on us. And for most of them, we still have a chance to recover from them.

Aim to do Your Best and be Happy About the Output

In most cases, the outcome of a task is out of your control. Regardless of how well you do the task, there are always unforeseen factors that may come into play that will affect its chance of success.

Because this factor is not always within our control, being obsessed with them all the time is of no use. Instead, you should just think about doing your best with all the tasks that are asked of you.

Doing your best does not mean that you become complacent with how you handle your tasks. It means that you should be critical of your performance rather than the outcome of the task. When preparing a report, make sure that all sections of the report are done properly. Do not think of what your boss would think about the report. Instead, focus on what you could do right now to make the output better.

By focusing on how well you do the process instead of the outcome of the task, you will lessen your fear of failure. Focus on what you need to do and the steps that you need to take. Try to clear your mind of other types of thoughts. Only think of what you need to do next.

Try to Develop a Healthier Lifestyle to Get More Energy

Procrastinators also tend to delay working on their health. They always say that they will start eating healthy and sleeping on time. In the end, however, they do not create plans that will help them achieve this. This, in turn, leads them to live an unhealthy lifestyle.

An unhealthy lifestyle usually leads to low energy at work. As discussed above, lousy eating and resting habits make a person lethargic. When a person feels that his energy reserves are weak, they are more likely to give in to his procrastination.

To overcome this, you need to eat at the proper times of the day so that you have the energy to start working. People working on a nine-to-five schedule should eat a big breakfast.

They should also take the time to eat lunch and small dinner 2-3 hours before going to sleep. This eating pattern will ensure that you will have enough energy to go about your day.

You should also add some time and money allocated to snacking. At times, the period between meals can be too long. You may feel low on energy and hungry before the next meal time. You can give yourself an energy boost by taking healthy snacks.

Aside from timing your meals, you should also make sure that you only take in high quality and healthy foods. The only way to ensure this is to prepare your meals; every person should learn to prepare their meals. By doing so, you will always know what types of ingredients and nutrients you put into your food. Relying on fast food, or pre-packaged junk food from the shop is a bad habit to have as this food is not as nutritionally balanced and contains a lot of fat and additional preservatives that are bad for your health and energy levels.

To ensure that you have the energy for the tasks that you set out to do, you should make sure that you take in a decent amount of carbohydrates, protein, and fats as recommended by nutrition experts. However, you should not overeat at once. When we overeat, we often feel drowsy. This happens because the body redirects blood flow from the other organs towards our digestive system.

Our digestive system gets the majority of the energy flowing into our bloodstream. Our other organs temporarily feel the effect of this process. One of the organs affected is the brain. Because of the lower levels of glucose and oxygen going into the brain, you start to feel sleepy. Many people want to rest after they have eaten because they feel drowsy. They do not want to start working until they get enough downtime. This is why if you have a large lunch, you can often feel lethargic in the afternoon.

You can avoid this by being smart with the amount of food you take in. Instead of eating three big meals in a day, you should aim to eat six or smaller meals. This way, you still take in the same amount of food, but you limit the tendency of feeling sleepy after a meal. This will help you become fitter to work on your tasks even after your meals.

> **NOTE:** If you are on a calorie restricted or specialized diet that has been recommended by your doctor, then that doctors' advice overrides any advice given in this book.

Go to Bed Earlier

You should also get enough sleep to make sure that your mind is ready and alert during your working hours. If you have trouble sleeping, you should make it a priority to establish your sleeping habits on work nights during the week.

If you need to be at work by nine, you need to make sure that you wake up early so that you will have enough time to do all the necessary preparations at home and still have enough time for your drive or commute to your work. You need to consider factors like traffic to make sure that you get to your workplace on time.

You can only ensure that you will have enough time for all of these if you get enough sleep. To achieve this, you will need to sleep for six to eight hours before your actual waking time. If you wish to wake up at seven in the morning, then you need to make sure that you sleep before 11 PM the previous night. This means that you need to stop all your tasks and start preparing for bed at 10:30 PM or earlier.

If you are not accustomed to sleeping early, you should do some tasks in your day that will make you feel tired by the time your bedtime arrives. You could work out at the gym or do work that requires you to move. By spending more energy than you usually do in a day, you will increase the likelihood that you will be tired when it's bedtime.

You should also avoid eating and drinking caffeinated food and beverages late in the day. Put all your coffee and cola intakes at the beginning of your day so that they will not affect your sleeping pattern. I tend to drink normal caffeinated tea and coffee in the morning and switch to decaffeinated coffee in the afternoon.

This does all become much harder though if you are a parent to young children. Being a parent, it is common to have broken sleep, especially when your children are very young. While getting lots of rest is what you want to aim for, the reality can be much tougher, but this makes having a healthy diet all the more important when you are trying to focus on your work.

Reduce Screen Time Before Bedtime

You will also feel like sleeping at your designated bedtime if you reduce the amount of stimulation that your brain gets. Most insomniacs do not know that some types of tasks keep their mind active even when they are about to sleep.

Using digital devices has this kind of effect on our brain. When you use social networking apps or play mobile games on your phone, you program your mind to keep being active even when you are about to sleep. If this becomes a habit, you will have a difficult time sleeping during your scheduled bedtime.

Many of the things we do on our phones are also designed to become addictive. The games and apps on your phone make money if you spend more time using them. The developers of these apps want you to keep coming back and keep using their apps.

To do this, they hire people who are trained and experienced in manipulating the behavior of people through the use of behavioral learning theories. They use reward systems and feel-good mechanisms to make sure that you become hooked on their games and their apps.

If you start using a particular game or app before you sleep, you are more likely to miss your scheduled sleeping time. People who play games or browse through social media usually end up spending more time on these apps than they intended. They end up sacrificing their rest time to use these apps instead of sleeping restfully.

You are more likely to succeed in establishing your habits if you limit your use of digital devices right before you sleep. Instead of keeping your face glued to the screen, you could read a book. You will eventually become tired and sleepy after reading enough chapters.

If you develop reading into a habit before you sleep, your brain will eventually become conditioned to become sleepy when you read books. This will make the sleeping process more comfortable for you.

Chapter 3 - A Step-by-Step Process in Beating Procrastination

You do not need to make the process of ending your procrastination habit difficult. In this section, we will discuss the steps that you could take to stop this habit. These measures give you a systematic approach to deal with the procrastination problem.

Learn Why You Are Procrastinating

Procrastination can be a sign that there is something wrong with the task that you are doing or the way it is managed. It is possible that you are procrastinating because your personality does not match the job that you are doing. Let's say that you are an extrovert and your boss is asking you to do all your tasks alone, with no interactions with other people. Because of the lack of human interactions, you do not enjoy the work at all.

Some people only procrastinate on the task when they are overworked. This could happen when your boss or your teachers give you too many things to do in a limited time. When we are overworked, our body does not get enough rest. Because of the lack of energy, we tend to choose and put off the important tasks.

You should learn your specific reason why you procrastinate. The sooner you know the real reason why, the faster it will be for you to find a solution.

Find the Obstacles to Productivity

Now that you know why you procrastinate, the next step is to learn about the obstacles stopping you from becoming productive. You may procrastinate because the office environment is too noisy. In this case, the noise is preventing you from doing your work, so you procrastinate on your work until the obstacle has gone.

Obstacles are the factors in the environment and your mind that lead to your procrastination. In the car sales industry, it is common for store managers to require their salespeople to do cold calls. This is the practice of calling prospective clients to invite them to come to the shop and purchase a new car.

Because of the intrusive nature of the activity, many salespeople put this task off. Instead of starting to do this task early in the month to maximize its effect, people often begin working on it only when they are already behind their sales quota. In this case, the procrastination is caused by a mental factor, the fear for the task itself.

Procrastination is also typical in the work-at-home industry. Workers in this sector tend to procrastinate on their tasks because of different types of obstacles or distractions in their way at home. I work from home, and this is something I have to be careful and aware of.

For most people in this industry, environmental aspects also affect their productivity other than the mental issue. For many of them, the presence of the comforts at home may be too inviting to ignore. When they see the couch in front of the TV, they are reminded of their habit of sitting on that couch when they are relaxing. Now that they work at home, nothing is stopping them from actually doing that regularly.

It may also be the lack of a boss that is causing them to procrastinate. They do not have a person breathing down their necks to pressure them to do the work. People who transition to this kind of job tend to become intoxicated with their new-found freedom. Instead of using their time wisely, they choose to be idle anytime they want. This leads to lower productivity. In this case, the obstacle is the lack of a motivating human figure.

To remedy your procrastination habit, you will need to find out what the obstacles are in your day-to-day activities that tend to distract you from your tasks and lead you to procrastinate. It could be a mental factor, or it can be an environmental factor that discourages you from doing the task.

In some cases, it could be a social factor. If you hate your boss, you may just want to rebel against his orders, and this leads you to knowingly delay doing the tasks that you need to be doing.

Whatever the obstacles are, you need to identify them first before you can start doing anything to stop procrastinating. One way to track the barriers preventing you from being productive is by observing your working environment. If you work in an office, try to identify the factors in there that serve as productivity obstacles. It could be the noise in the room or the subtler factors like the temperature or humidity.

If it is an environmental factor, the best strategy is to change the venue of your workplace. This simple step will remove all the productivity obstacles in your way. If it is not possible to move your tasks somewhere else, then you have no other choice but to work on the barriers one by one.

You can deal with the noise by using noise canceling headphones. You could also deal with the visual distractions by facing away from them when you are working. By blocking out these environmental distractions, your mind will be clearer, and you will be able to focus on your tasks. I wear a set of Bose QC35 noise canceling headphones when I am working. They are fantastic at helping to block out your environment. I also wear them when traveling as it cuts down the sound of train or plane engines.

After identifying the environmental distractions, you will need to start checking the mental factors that are preventing you from becoming productive. This includes distracting thoughts that are preventing you from focusing on the job.

Fear is the most common mental factor. Most of the time, we have subtle fears of the task that we need to do. Our fears paralyze us from working. An adverse reaction to fear is to run away from it. All types of fear trigger a common response in our brain. In the previous section, we discussed how the fight or flight responses are used by the brain to deal with fear. It is essential for you to avoid making a habit of choosing the flight response.

Whenever you choose this option, and you become satisfied with it, the subconscious mind figuratively takes notes on the success of the strategy. The mind learns that using this response is useful in dealing with these types of sources of fear. The next time you feel fear or anxiety, the mind tells you to take the same flight response.

The same anti-fear mechanism works against difficult tasks. If we choose to run away from the source of the fear, we will develop a habit of using the flight response even for unthreatening sources of fear like seemingly tricky tasks.

In the beginning, you may have told yourself that you will only miss the task once. You tell yourself that the procrastination will only be temporary and that you will do your best tomorrow. However, unknown to you that your brain has picked up the behavior as a successful flight response. Because the flight response is successful, your mind will invoke the same thought patterns in the future when you encounter the same source of fear.

Your subconscious mind though is not always in control. Now that you know how the fight or flight mechanism works, you are more equipped with the knowledge to avoid the same habits from taking control of your behavior in the future.

Knowing that the flight response leads to procrastination, you need to choose to fight the source of the fear actively.

Getting Rid of the Obstacles

As you start to examine your behavior and the critical factors surrounding it, you will realize that many factors will lead to procrastination. In this step, you will need to get rid of the ones that you can; by doing this, you will minimize the number of distractions that will take your mind away from the task at hand.

We have already discussed some of the possible strategies that may work for you when getting rid of the obstacles. For environmental factors, you can begin by transferring your workplace to somewhere else with fewer distractions.

You will need to find a solution for each of the important productivity obstacles in your way. Here is a list of categories of the strategies on how you could do this.

Avoidance

The first option is to avoid the distraction altogether. This strategy can be applied in many scenarios, and it is the best among the categories of approach because it is the least stressful. To use this strategy, you simply need to move away from the source of the distraction so that you will be able to do your work.

To make this type of strategy work, you will need to anticipate when the distraction will come and take the necessary steps to avoid it before that time arrives. When trying to work at home, for instance, we often become distracted by the different things going on around us. The kids may be too loud, the neighbor may be too noisy, or the lure of watching Netflix becomes too high.

To avoid these types of obstacles, you can choose to do your work at a time when they are not present. You could choose to wake up earlier than the people around you and start working on your tasks, or you could spend some time in a local coffee shop to remove yourself from the distractions completely. By doing so, you can focus on your tasks better without getting bothered by the distractions.

Blocking

The second option is to block off the distractions. This is the next best option if avoiding the obstacles is not possible. In this option, we try various methods to prevent our senses from detecting the distractions or obstacles. When the noise around you is the reason for your procrastination, and you cannot move away from it, the next best option is to block the noise.

As suggested earlier, you can use a noise canceling headphones to deal with this kind of problem. You could then choose the types of music that will not distract you from your work. In cases like these, music with no words/lyrics is the best style to listen to because it is often the words in the song that distract us from putting our full attention on the task at hand. I love to listen to movie scores. I am a fan of the genre, and there are no words to distract you. I have an extensive playlist of over 9 hours of music, and I just randomly shuffle through the playlist. I also find ambient music as a great style of music to listen to as it just fades into the background while blocking out external noises.

Satisfaction

Some types of obstacles cannot be avoided or blocked. Hunger is a good example. For these kinds of obstacles, the best strategy is to satisfy the need that causes the distraction. Just like with the first strategy, you will need to anticipate this type of obstacle and prevent it from happening by satisfying the needs that correspond with, i.e., get something to eat if you are hungry. Be careful not to confuse hunger with being thirsty though. If you are dehydrated, you can sometimes misread the signal as hunger. I always keep a bottle of water next to me when I am working and sip it regularly.

Let's say that you tend to procrastinate when you are hungry. You could prepare for this distraction by scheduling your meals so that it does not happen to you again. This strategy mostly applies to getting rid of physiological distractions. However, it could also apply when dealing with people. A parent could prepare all the needs of their kids for school before working on their tasks. This way, the kids will not bother them when they are working.

Confrontation

The last and probably most stressful response to an obstacle is to confront it. If a co-worker is noisy, you could choose to ask them to stop so that you can work in peace. With this method, you will need to face the source of the obstacle to have the distraction removed. By removing the obstacles related to your work, you will have fewer distractions around you, and this will allow you to work continuously.

Just Start with the Task

Now that you have removed all the anticipated obstacles in your path, it's time to start doing the task. This, however, is easier said than done. In the beginning, you may need to force yourself to do the right thing. Let's say you need to find a new job. In the beginning, your mind will try to resist the tasks involved with this goal. This is because you are not accustomed to doing these tasks, or you fear rejection from the job applications.

For some of us, the task of going to interviews and meeting new people make us anxious. Because of these uncomfortable feelings associated with the task, the mind will try to avoid it.

However, to overcome procrastination, you will need to resist the urge of taking the easy road. It is hard at the beginning when you do the tasks for the first few times. However, as you gain experience in doing a particular type of task, you also gain confidence in doing it.

It's just like riding a bike. In the beginning, you feel anxious in doing it. You begin by riding slowly and cautiously. After doing it a few times, you eventually develop the confidence in doing it. After spending hours riding the bike, it feels natural to you. If you keep facing the source of your fears, it will eventually become a habit for you. You will no longer be afraid of the task.

A habit is a set of tasks that we do as a part of our routine. To develop a habit, you will need to understand how they work. We will discuss this in the following chapters.

Chapter 4 – Refining your Work Habits

You need to learn how to become better at resisting procrastination. One way to do this is by establishing working habits that prevent procrastination from happening in the first place.

Components of a Habit

Habits form naturally even without your intervention. If you drink soda every day before you leave work, you will notice that you'll start to crave for the drink at the same time every day. Because there is little resistance with this task, the habit of drinking a soda at this particular time of the day is formed naturally.

Habit creation does not happen by chance. For a habit to form naturally, it first needs to have all the necessary components.

Most natural habits are formed when two factors are present, the task and the reward. The task is the set of activities that you do to complete the habit. As a result, for doing these activities, you are given a reward. In the beginning, the task is not yet a part of your routine. For these factors to be included in your routine, you should keep doing them on a regular basis.

The habit usually comes with a trigger. This is a signal that tells us that it is time to do the task. Your morning routine starts with the alarm clock. When the clock makes its sound, you start a series of actions that lead to the completion of the routine on a daily basis.

You may say that not all people who use an alarm clock have a successful morning routine. Some people continue to sleep when the alarm sounds while others hit the snooze button instead of getting up immediately.

We can generally say that there are two types of people based on how they respond to their alarm clocks. The first type gets up and starts the day immediately after they hear the alarm go off. The other type tells themselves that they still have time to sleep some more. As a response, they set the clock for five more minutes.

This shows that habits do not always form as we intend them to be.

Why do two different routines follow the same trigger?

It is important to remember that the tasks that you most often do and the ones that you most prefer doing end up becoming habits. If you prefer to hit the snooze button most of the time, then that practice will most likely lead to becoming the habit. If you prefer to wake up early and just start with your tasks, then this activity will become your habit instead.

To create productive habits, you will need to put all your attention into the process in the beginning. By giving the habit-forming process more of your attention, you will be able to control how it forms.

Creating a Habit

You will be able to prevent procrastination efficiently if you set your essential tasks to become habits. They can only become habits if you start with the proper mindset of maintaining focus and aiming for maximum productivity.

Let's begin with how you can create this mindset.

The Productivity Mindset

To be able to fend off procrastination, you will need to aim for productivity as your highest priority. To do this, let us first start by defining what productivity is for you.

Productivity has a different meaning for every person. For someone who is single trying to climb the corporate ladder, productivity may include all the tasks that have to be achieved to get a promotion. For this person, they will spend most of their time working on the critical projects in their job and meeting the right people so that they will be considered for a promotion when one is up for grabs.

On the other hand, for someone with a family with three school-aged kids, productivity may refer to the completion of tasks that increases their income. To be able to provide for all the needs of their family, this person takes on multiple jobs to maximize the amount of income they get each day.

To beat procrastination, you should first define what productivity means to you. If you do not know what it means, then you will need to take some time to think about it. As you start to get older, you will start to realize the things and the people that you value the most. These factors will help you learn how to create your definition of productivity.

Set Your Goals

To accurately define the tasks that make you productive, you will first need to state your personal goals. To keep it simple, you could start by listing down all the 20 things that you want to achieve in your life. Each person's list differs, depending on what they want to achieve.

When setting goals, it is important to remember to keep them realistic. If some of the goals in your list seem unrealistic, you should remove them from your list. You should also make sure that your goals are specific enough to be measured. They should also include a deadline so that you will know when will the goal start and when will it end.

You could remove some of the goals you listed that do not have these characteristics. You can also rephrase some of them. By the end of the process, your list of goals will be shorter, and they are better designed so that you can start working on them right away.

After creating your goals, arrange them according to how you want to prioritize them. Naturally, more important goals should be higher on the list, the topmost being the most important. By arranging your goals according to their importance, you will be able to know which tasks need to be prioritized.

Setting Tasks to Your Goals

Goals are only valuable if you work on them. To reach them, you need to assign tasks to them. Ideally, you should already know which tasks lead to the completion of your goals. If not, you will need to do your research. You could begin by searching the web on the process of how you can achieve the goal. Also look up if there are good books written about the process or goal that you want to achieve.

Books usually provide more details as to how you can achieve your goals. The information in books is organized, and they typically offer the essential steps on how you can achieve your goals. Aside from this, you could also look into blogs of people who tried to accomplish the same goal. By finding people who tried to do the same goal, you will be able to prove that it is possible for you to achieve it.

When researching, it may be handy if you have a note-taking tool. You can use a pen and a notebook or a notetaking app; I use Microsoft OneNote. You should write down the steps involved in reaching your chosen goal. You could also take down the essential tips that you find in your research.

When you do your research, you should prioritize the goals that are on the top of your list first. These goals are supposed to be the most important goals for you. If you find yourself gravitating towards the goals in the lower parts of the list, this could mean one of two things.

First, you may have misarranged your goals on your list. It is possible that some of the important goals in your list are ranked lower than they should be. Second, it is possible that you are procrastinating on your more important tasks. If this is the correct reason, then you have ranked the goals correctly.

However, because the goals at the top of your list aren't easy to achieve, you may be avoiding them to get to the accessible parts of the list. If this is the case, then you will need to motivate yourself to work on the more important tasks first.

Identify Tasks That can be Turned into Habits

Some of your top goals contain tasks that require being repeated over and over again. If your goal is to lose weight, you will need to work out 3-5 times a week. You will also need to go on a weekly trip to shop for the right types of food. The only way to work efficiently on these tasks is by developing habits. You can start doing this by putting each task in a designated time slot.

Start by identifying the best time to make the habit. For working out, the best time may be early in the morning after you wake up. This way, your workout will help boost your metabolism for the rest of the day. You could then schedule your food shopping task at the end of your day on your way home.

When deciding on the best time to do a task, you should make sure that you consider when you will be able to do the task successfully. If you think that working out in the morning is too tricky for you, it may be better to schedule this task at another time when it will be easier for you to do the workout.

After scheduling your tasks that will be turned into habits, the next step is to identify the trigger and the rewards that will come with the habit. It will be significantly easier for you to build the habit if it comes with a trigger and a reward.

As stated earlier, the trigger should serve as a signal to start the habit. For natural habits like eating, the trigger is hunger or craving for a specific type of food. The trigger should remind you of the needs that the habit helps to satisfy.

For one of your goals, you could set an alarm clock to go off five minutes before the schedule of the habit. To remind yourself of how important the habit is, look at how important it is with your goal. You can do this by going back to your list of goals. By reminding yourself of your goal every time, you will be able to motivate yourself to do them and not procrastinate.

When the time to start the habit arrives, just start doing it. Do not overthink the process. It is common for procrastinators to overthink, like looking for alternatives for the task at hand.

Put a Place and a Time in Your Habit

You can prevent yourself from procrastinating on these types of tasks by designating a specific time for them. To do this, you need to choose a date and a time for your task. Ideally, you should put it in a timeslot wherein you will not be tempted to do anything else.

If your task is to learn to play the guitar, you should put it in a timeslot where you are not busy. You could schedule it right after your working hours. This will allow you to do something during rush hour so that you do not have to deal with the excessive traffic on the road.

After selecting a suitable timeslot for your task, find a designated place for it. Ideally, you should do this new task also in a new place. If you put it in a place that you are already familiar with, you are likely to fall into your old habits and patterns of behavior. If you choose to do your work at home, you are in danger of procrastinating on the task and doing some of the old habits.

Instead of working on your task to develop a new habit, you may choose to set it aside to do other less important tasks like watching TV or surfing the web. Building your habit will be easier when you put it in the same place and time and if you do it regularly.

Remind Yourself of Your Goal

In this part of the process, you will need to choose a tool that will help you keep track of your goal and your next tasks. You can stop yourself from procrastinating if you could keep reminding yourself of what you are trying to achieve. You should also have a way to keep track your progress and of the next steps in your plan. In this section, we will talk about the different tools you can use to record your progress.

Creating a Workflow Outline

A workflow is simply a list wherein you can put all the steps in your project or task. With a workflow outline, you will be able to keep track of the major steps in your task and the smaller steps within each task.

A basic workflow outline lists the major steps in a project like follows

Example:

> Step 1
>
> Step 2
>
> Step 3

You could then add smaller tasks inside these major stages. You could use small letters to organize these smaller steps:

Example:

> Step 1
>
>> Step 1.1
>>
>> Step 1.2
>>
>> Step 1.3
>
> Step 2
>
> Step 3

This type of workflow is simple, and it is easy to use. Anyone with a piece of paper and a pen can do it. If you use this method, you could then mark the steps that you have finished with a check mark. This way, you will always know what the next step is.

Using a Goal Setting App

There are lots of various goal setting apps that are on the market today which can help you keep track of the ones you set. The features in these apps vary depending on the developer. You could check these apps and see if they will work for you.

If you are planning to do something specific, there may also be goal setting apps for specific purposes. If your goal is to lose weight, there are many goal setting and tracking apps for this purpose that you can download for free online. I will be talking about software that I use to help with maintaining focus later in the book, but a tool I personally use for recording goals is Trello.

Using a Journal

Journals allow you to keep records of your goals and keep track of your progress. Journaling is a unique discipline all in itself. You will need a single notebook that will serve as your journal. Ideally, your journal should only contain one type of content. If your goal is about exercising and dieting, you should keep your journal content to that goal.

With a journal, you will be able to keep your mind to become aware of how you are progressing with your goal. In your journal, you should include all the details about your experience in trying to reach your goal and getting rid of your procrastination habit. By putting your experience onto paper, you will be able to document your journey. This can be useful when you meet challenges along the way. You can use your experience as documented in the journal to guide your future decision-making process. I keep an electronic journal for recording what I am up to. The journal I use is a service called Penzu which I highly recommend.

Chapter 5 – Developing your Ability to Focus

Being able to focus is an ability to keep your mind on a specific task for a period. We are required to focus on a variety of reasons. When someone is speaking, we are usually required to give our undivided attention; this is just one form of concentrating. When we study, we are also required to focus. However, the strategy for listening to someone speaking is different from the approach needed for studying.

Your ability to focus depends on your motivation to complete a task. For some types of tasks, keeping our focus is easy. A child playing video games can focus on the game for hours without getting distracted. However, when it comes to studying, the same child fails to focus on the task for even just ten minutes.

In this chapter, we will talk about how you can improve your ability to focus on the task that you need to do. To enhance your ability to focus, you will need to plan and prepare for the task.

Plan Your Strategy for Your Tasks

Before you can start working on your task, you should first plan for it. When you do your planning, you need to define what level of work you will put in your task. Some types of tasks require intensive thinking while others require a lot of physical effort from you. Other tasks also need you only to show up. For these types of tasks, you are giving up time instead of physical or mental effort.

Aside from identifying the type of effort that you will put into the task, you should also think about the finished product. You should define what it will be like when the task is done. What are the requirements that you need to comply with so that you will be done with the task within the given time? For most of us, these requirements are set by somebody else. It may be dictated by the boss or by a client that we are working with.

To avoid procrastination, you will need to work continuously to comply with these requirements. By defining what the finished product looks like to you, you will remove the uncertainty that comes with the task. You will know what you will need to do and to accomplish, decreasing the anxiety in your mind.

For some types of task, there will be no defined result. If you want to start a business, the tasks involved are related to building an efficient and effective money-making system rather than to create any specific product. These tasks tend to have no deadline, and there is no one there to tell us what elements need to be present in the result.

To plan for these types of tasks, you need to define what success means to you with this task personally. Sometimes, it is necessary to break down the entire process into smaller projects. In the case of starting a business, the first project will be the business planning and conceptualization stage. In this stage, the future business owner decides on what he wants to offer as either a product or service. It may also be necessary to start planning for the business's marketing strategy and logistical features.

The process of building a business requires many other tasks, and these tasks will be dealt with in the future. For now, the business owner should only focus his attention on the current task.

You could also do the same with your tasks that do not have a defined deadline and result. Try to break it down into smaller stages and treat each of these stages as small projects that will lead to the big one. You need to set your criteria for success as well as the project's scope and limitations. This includes factors like your deadline.

In your planning, you should also create a list of what you need for the task. Before you do a specific step in your list of tasks, collect all the things that you need for that step first. By making sure that everything you need is already available, you will prevent delays when you are working. You will no longer stop your progress just to look for something around the house. Instead, all the things you need will be in front of you ready to be used.

If possible, you could also assign the job to a specific place. When planning for particular tasks that you will keep doing for a while, consider appointing a specific workplace for it. If you need to study for a long exam, why not find a place where you can do it consistently without being disturbed. Instead of just doing it in your room or wherever you land inside the house, consider going to the local library to study.

By assigning a special place for this task, you will be able to make it easier for yourself to avoid distraction. When you go to the designated place for the task, you will be able to clear your mind of other distractions easily. You will instantly put your mind in the mood for working on the task at hand.

Ideally, you should choose a place suited for the task. Don't use a place where you already spend a lot of time. Working in your bedroom is often a bad idea because you associate the area with activities like sleeping; you will be tempted to do other things while you are in there.

If the task requires a lot of mental work, like studying, try to find a place with few features that stimulate the senses. Look for a quiet place where there are not a lot of movements.

You can also find a place where other people go to do the same task as yours. When trying to focus on losing weight, you can choose to run on the local trail. In this place, the people you meet are also running on the trail. You will not be distracted by their presence because they are in the same mindset as you.

If you are in a park, the people you meet there are not necessarily doing the same activity as you. Some of them may be having fun or eating while you are running your lap. Their presence will distract you from keeping your mind focused on the task that you are doing. When I really need to focus, I often go to my local coffee shop. During the day, I quite often see lots of people sitting there with laptops working. I find the ambiance of the coffee shop a great way to focus on what I am doing. I can normally be more productive at here in 2 hours than I can be working from home for double that amount of time.

Prepare Yourself for the First Steps

Procrastination is a habit and breaking it can be challenging. I would be lying to you if I told you that you would end your procrastination habit immediately after reading this book. It does not work like that. It took you a long time to build your habit of procrastination. Most of us start doing it since we were in grade school. It would be unrealistic to expect that it will be gone within a day or two.

There is no kill switch or magic spell that will automatically turn your procrastination habit off. The best strategy to remove it from your daily routine is to take control of your daily behavior and activities actively. There should no longer be any passive action towards this habit. When we act passively, we let our natural tendencies decide what our efforts will be. We allow our old habits rule our daily behavior. This practice needs to go if you want to beat procrastination.

You will need to expect, however, that the first steps will not be easy. It usually takes a regular procrastinator multiple goes before they can stop their old tendencies. You will need to acknowledge that you will also experience the same thing. Prepare yourself emotionally for the failure of your first few attempts.

A key component for beating procrastination is scheduling your tasks and following through; many people can plan their tasks with no problem. It's in the follow-through where most people fail. Because they are not used to pushing themselves to work without a deadline, most people fighting procrastination tend to suffer in this step.

You may also experience the same thing. If you have been a chronic procrastinator all your life, you will probably have not enough willpower to push yourself out of your old habits. Because this part is inevitable, the best strategy against it is to be emotionally prepared to carry on. If you fail to follow through on your plans to stop procrastinating today, do not beat yourself up about it.

Forgive yourself and focus your attention towards making the necessary adjustments to become successful tomorrow. You will only fail if you give up on it. If you keep on trying, you will eventually build the resolve to fight your urges to start procrastinating.

Refine Your Methods After Each Failure

When you fail with the execution of your plans and you end up procrastinating again, you will need to make the necessary adjustments that will ensure that you will not fail again in your future attempts. Not giving up on the process is just the first step. To succeed, you will need to make the necessary adjustments.

Take Alan, for example. He has been planning to start working out since he last saw his medical test results. He prepared all the things he needed to work out on, and he set the workout session in his schedule. All he has to do is to do the task when his alarm clock tells him that it is time.

In his last attempt, he failed to follow through with his planning. While he was waiting for the time to work out, he started playing video games. When the alarm clock sounded, he is no longer in the mood to work out. Instead, he just kept playing video games, and he told himself that he would start working out tomorrow.

This is a classic case of procrastination. Instead of working out, Alan chose to do the more comfortable and less stressful activity, and that is playing video games. To become successful in the future, Alan will need to adjust his methods so that the factors that led to his procrastination in the past will no longer be present. He could change the location of his workout session. This way, there will be fewer distractions around him. He will be able to focus his attention on the task to be done.

You will also experience setbacks similar to the example above. At times, you will fail in resisting your old procrastination habits. You can still succeed in your future attempts if you just find the right adjustments in your method.

How to Give Your 100%

Genuinely focused individuals can go all out on their tasks. They know which tasks need the highest levels of focus and they know how to manage their time and energy so that they can work with maximum effectiveness and efficiency on the task.

Identify the Task That Requires 100% Focus

Not all the tasks on your to-do list require your 100% attention. This level of care puts stress on your mind, and it requires high levels of willpower. Because of this, you need to limit this type of effort only to your most important tasks.

For some of us, we only put this level of attention on our career-boosting tasks. This includes office work and other career-related tasks. Others put 100% effort on jobs that lead to professional and personal development. They apply their highest level of focus on tasks like attending classes for higher education or reading books and practicing what they've learned.

You will need to choose your task where you will put 100% of your focus. This task should be important to you and the time and effort that you invest in it should lead to significant future returns.

By choosing only one project or task to put your 100% effort on, you will be able to excel in one area of your life, without sacrificing too much. You will still have time for other important aspects of family and personal growth.

In contrast, choosing to maximize your efforts on more than one project at a time may stretch out your time and effort too thinly, and it may exhaust you. Burnout is the leading cause of mediocrity and procrastination in the workplace. Overworked people usually feel that the efforts they put into their jobs are underappreciated. Because of this, their enthusiasm towards their work is negatively affected. Poor morale in the workforce can lead to bad habits like procrastination.

You should only choose one task where you will give it your all at this time. When you are done with this task, you can do other tasks that will require the same level of attention.

Build a Personal System

You will need to actively change your routine to be able to achieve 100% effectiveness and efficiency. To start, you first need to identify the tasks that you need to do. Just like in earlier activities, you should also define the requirements for success for this particular task or project.

After this, you should start scheduling your tasks. By planning when you will start working, you will create the prototype of your success system. Consider this plan as the first of many iterations that will happen in the future. In this schedule or plan, you aim to get one hundred percent effectiveness from each working day. By 100% effectiveness, we mean that you will keep working and focusing on the task until you have achieved the goal for the day or until you need rest.

To build your system, you should plot your working times throughout your day, giving your chosen task the highest priority. You will need to schedule these tasks at the times of the day when you are most effective. People are more effective in the morning once they have woken up with their morning coffee; they are rested after a full night's sleep, and they are ready to do their tasks.

If you are also most active and effective in your work at this time in the morning, you could schedule to do the bulk of your work during these hours. The most critical tasks in your chosen project should fall in this section of your day.

A procrastinator usually achieves very little at the beginning of the day. Many people procrastinate at this time by doing menial and unimportant tasks like talking to co-workers or checking emails. You should check your behavior if you tend to do the same. When you catch yourself doing a trivial task at this time, you should stop yourself and redirect your effort in your chosen task.

Luckily, this is also the time of the day when our willpower is at its best. Willpower is your mind's ability to redirect the body's effort towards the tasks that are important to us. With enough willpower, we can push ourselves to avoid unimportant tasks. This allows us to stop procrastinating. At times, it also allows us to work for more extended periods or at a higher intensity than planned.

Experts now believe that willpower is usually the strongest when we are well-rested and when we have eaten well. It is often the strongest in the morning. Because of multiple factors, our willpower tends to decrease as the day goes on. Some experts suggest that the more difficult decisions we make throughout the day, the more our willpower depletes.

Other factors also affect our willpower such as fatigue, hunger, drowsiness and the anticipation at the end of the workday. When our mind is focused on at least one of these factors, our willpower starts to fail. At this point, old habits tend to overcome our higher level of thinking skills.

Knowing that there is a limit in your willpower, you should schedule your most difficult and important tasks early in the morning when you are still highly enthusiastic about your work.

Build Around Your Essential Tasks

Now that you have scheduled your essential tasks, you should start considering the other tasks that you need to do. You need to plan your less critical tasks so that they will adjust to your scheduled prioritized tasks.

First off, you need to identify the tasks that you can delegate to other people. If you have someone to do simple errands for you, you will be able to decrease the number of things that you need to worry about. Less essential tasks such as picking up the dry cleaning or buying groceries can be easily delegated to someone else.

After removing tasks that can be delegated, your next task is to assign a schedule to the tasks that you need to do yourself. When assigning a plan to these less critical tasks, put them in the timeslots wherein they do not conflict with your prioritized tasks.

Start Right After Planning

Most people rest immediately after planning something as if they've just accomplished something significant. To avoid using planning as a procrastination method, you should put a lesser value on the act of planning. Planning, by itself, is worthless. This activity should be partnered with an immediate effort to add value to it.

You should plan your schedule right after your planning session as well. If you are sitting at your desk to plan at nine in the morning, your next activity after that should be around 9:15 or 9:30. This will ensure that you will not waste time doing excessive planning. This will also guarantee that you will start becoming productive immediately right after the planning session.

Start Small

To make big projects less intimidating, try to aim only for small levels of success when you are starting out. Procrastinators usually start their habit when they feel anxious about the task that they need to do. Often, it is the amount of work required by the task that makes it intimidating.

To lessen the anxiety, you could aim for smaller goals. When you do this, you are encouraging yourself just to start working. Instead of working for 5 hours straight, you could start working for one hour only. Surely, you will be able to stick to a task this short.

After working the task for an hour, you could choose to take a 5-10-minute rest. This part is optional. If you think that you do not need to rest at this point, you could want to continue working for another hour. A conventional technique for this is called the Pomodoro technique where you work flat out for 20 minutes. This means no distractions, email, or phone at that time. You work as hard as you can and then take a 5-10-minute break. I will be talking about the Pomodoro technique at the end of this book when I discussed some tools you can use to help you.

Some tasks are more focused on other metrics aside from time. A salesperson is required to make 50 sales calls in a day. Instead of aiming to do ten calls in the first hour, he could intend to do just the first one at this time. It will be significantly easier for him to convince himself to do only one call. If that call ends fast, he could use the momentum to dial the number of the next person on the list without thinking about it.

Stop Overthinking the Process

Now that the time for planning and strategizing is over, you should focus your mental power only on the task. You should not allow your thoughts to cloud your judgment. Instead, you should use your thoughts only to focus on the next step.

You could keep your mind focused on the task at hand by narrating the steps that you are taking. When you are forced to write a report for your boss, say the steps that you are taking so that your mind will be occupied. With an occupied mind, you will be able to resist thoughts that may distract you from your task.

When you are in your office, you could narrate your actions like this:

> "Firstly, I will turn on the computer. After that, I will open the word processor and write the letterhead. Next, I will write the greetings and the introduction of the letter…"

You could do this exercise in your mind. However, speaking your thoughts out loud will be more effective; although this is not always possible without you looking a little strange to your co-workers.

When you are stuck in one step of the process, you should step back from working and ask yourself, "What's next?"

By redirecting your thoughts like this, you will be able to have constant control over what you are thinking when you are supposed to be working. If your mind is not occupied when you are working, it is easier for distractions and thoughts of bailing out on the task to creep into it. The less developed parts of your brain will try to convince you to stop working and start resting.

You will need to resist these urges when they come. However, preventing them from redirecting your thoughts will allow you to stop these urges more consistently.

Clearing your Mind and Keeping It Relaxed

Your mind cannot be focused entirely if it is cluttered with all sorts of thoughts. The more concerns you have in your mind, the more potential distractions you also have. Each of your concerns has a chance of appearing in your thoughts and taking your attention away from your task. You will need to learn how to prevent these concerns from disturbing your progress.

You will need to train your mind to be constantly relaxed so that it can avoid your problems from affecting your ability to work. You can start to clear your mind through breathing exercises.

When you feel that you are stressed out, stand up straight and start breathing deeply. Do it 10 to 20 times until your mind is cleared. The more you do this activity, the better you will be at clearing your mind.

If the distracting thought requires action, take note of it and enter it into your schedule. As soon as you can work on it, do so. The more you push an unwanted task in the background, the stronger it grows. You will need to deal with the problem while it is still fresh.

Mindfulness and focus come together. Be mindful of the tasks that you need to do and the obstacles that are in your way, preventing you from accomplishing these tasks. If you are mindful of the big picture of your everyday activities, you will be able to create and implement better strategies on how to overcome challenges like procrastination.

Also, keep yourself mindful of your relaxation time. Your mind needs a constant dose of rest for it to be able to function at a high level continuously. To give the mind the relaxation it deserves, make sure that you sleep at the same time every night.

If you wake up at six in the morning, you should convince yourself to sleep at 10 or 11 in the evening. A well-planned sleeping pattern puts structure into your day and makes your routine more predictable. Keeping your schedule predictable helps your mind to remain relaxed.

You should also be mindful of how you spend your break time in between work sessions. During your lunch break, you should try to minimize the amount of stimulation that your senses get. For example, you could try to avoid using digital devices when you are resting.

In most cases, the multimedia experience of the internet puts stress on our mind. It forces our brain to work by reading the texts and watching videos. Even if you don't think that these activities are the same at work, your brain cannot distinguish the difference. To your brain, all these activities that stimulate our senses are considered work.

To keep your mind ready to work after your break, try to limit your mental activity when you are taking these short breaks. When eating a snack, try to keep your mind blank and keep your focus on the food that you are eating. Enjoy your meal without allowing your mind to wander off from one thought to another. By keeping your mind blank, you are truly resting it. Resting your mind will preserve your willpower and allow you to keep your focus on the task at hand.

Compartmentalize Your Thoughts

In line with keeping your mind clear from distractions, you should also try to compartmentalize your thoughts. Mental compartmentalization is the process of limiting the types of thoughts that you think of according to the tasks that you are doing. People who require high levels of focus like professional athletes, scientists, and world-class musical performers all use a variation of this method.

The idea is to identify the thoughts that enter your mind. If they are related to your task, you should continue to entertain it. Otherwise, you should remove it from your mind. When you are doing a project, for example, your thoughts should only be related to the project. You should not think about what you will do afterward, or any other activity not related to the task that you are doing now.

It may seem like common sense to keep your mind focused on the task at hand. You will be surprised, however, of how often people allow unimportant thoughts to disturb their chain of thought.

72

Compartmentalization should be practiced in all areas of your life. When you are bonding with your family, you should have no other thoughts on your mind other than the activity that you are doing. Your thoughts should be focused on the experience and the people that you are bonding with.

The same goes when you are resting. When in this state, you should not allow your mind to be cluttered with thoughts from work. Instead, you should follow the tips in the previous section and try to keep your mind clear.

There will be times when your mind will be too cluttered even when you try to keep it clear. When the breathing exercise we talked about in this chapter is no longer working, this may mean that you need to rest your mind. You should do this when you notice that your quality of work is already suffering because of the clutter in your mind.

When this happens, you could give yourself a five to ten-minute break to rest your mind. After removing all the stimulations in your mind in this period, the amount of clutter in your mind may lessen.

Track Progress and Refine your Process

You may not become successful in improving your productivity the first time around. Do not let this affect your enthusiasm towards your goals. Instead, you should try to find out why you failed to reach your goal. Ideally, you should look for a metric that will support your decision making.

If you are trying to lose weight and you failed to reach your goal, you should examine the process that you are using. It is possible that you are putting in the time, but the exercises that you are using are not intensive enough to help you lose those calories.

The issue could also be in your diet. The calories you lose in your workouts may just be canceled out by the number of calories you take in. You will need to examine the steps you are taking in your goal to improve your results in the future.

You should not give up on your goal just because you failed on your first try. Giving up can become a habit, and it can support your irrational fear of failure. You should keep your mind focused on the goal. Analyze your first attempt and find the areas where you can improve. Treat each of your failures as a learning opportunity.

As soon as you find the reason behind the failure, plan your approach again and give your goal a second try. You should make it a good habit to respond to failure this way so that you will not give in to the temptation of procrastinating again.

If you keep your mind focused on your goals and actively resisted procrastination, there is no doubt that you will become successful in reaching your goals.

Chapter 6 – Software Tools to Help?

In our modern world of technology, it is quite common for us to reach for digital tools to help us in our work. The act of searching for these tools can become a distraction in their own right and lead to much procrastination, but the right tools at the right time can help us. To save you the job of hunting for lots of tools, I have narrowed down a short list of tools that I use personally to help me with my daily work.

The specific tools themselves are not as important as the type of tools they are. By this I mean there are plenty of alternative tools on the market, but what is more important is what those tools do for you. I am an Apple Mac user, so the tools I am listing here are all on the Mac, but there are most likely alternatives on other platforms like Windows.

Before we look at the tools, I first want to point out that I am in no way affiliated with any of these tools or companies. I am writing about them as they are the tools I use and find helpful. In writing about them, I am hoping you will find them useful too.

Planning Tools

The first category of tools I use is to help with planning. As we have discussed in this book so far, planning should not be used as another form of procrastination, and over the years I have used some planning applications to help make the process easier and more efficient.

Trello

The first tool that I use daily is Trello which is available at https://trello.com. Trello is the primary tool I use to plan, organize and sort the day to day tasks that I need to do. The best way to think of Trello is that it is a list of lists contained within a board. As an example, I use three boards. I have the main board for my business where I prioritize and track progress on tasks. The 2nd board I use is for monitoring the various states of books I am writing, publishing and promoting. For me, it made sense to break the book tracking out into a separate board. The final board I use is for tracking home-based DIY and maintenance projects.

The boards that you create don't just have to be for your use. You can invite collaborators to a board, which makes this the perfect platform for team collaboration. With my home DIY board, I have my wife as a collaborator, which could just as easily be a team of people you are working with at the time. When I have worked for different small software development companies before, we used Trello to plan the work for the development team for a two-week sprint or iteration.

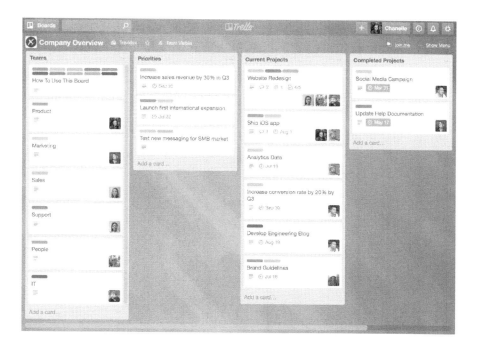

On the board, you will have different columns. The names of these columns are entirely up to you, but typically they might be used to monitor the state or progress of a task through different states. As an example, you might have the columns, Backlog, To-do, In-Progress, Done and Blocked. Tasks might start off in the Backlog column. This could be the big list of identified tasks that you need to work on. Then as you select some tasks for the day to work on, you drag them into the To-do column. You can drag the tasks into any order you like which could have the highest priority tasks at the top of the list.

As you start to work on a task, you can then drag the task into the In-Progress column. If the task gets blocked for any reason, such as you are waiting on some information, then you can pull it into the blocked column, or if you have completed the task, you then drag it into the Done column. This is just a simple example, but if you are tracking lots of tasks/tickets, then visualizing them on a board like this can be invaluable.

With each ticket on the board, you can also double-click on it to reveal more information. From here you can attach files, set and track checklists and add comments. This means each ticket on the board becomes a repository for information related to that ticket. This is helpful if you are collaborating on a board with someone else.

Trello can be run in your favorite web browser, but you also have the option to run it on iOS and Android phones as well as iOS and Android tablets. There are also native Windows and MacOS application that you can download and use. I use the MacOs version.

The best news also is that Trello is free to use. You do have a paid option which gives you some more features, but you don't need to pay for these if you don't want to.

Wunderlist

The next productivity tool that I use is Wunderlist which you can get from www.wunderlist.com. This is a more traditional To-Do list application in that you can have multiple lists to which you add To-Do items. This is my 2nd most used planning tool. I use this for straightforward To-Do reminders such as what I need to pack for a business trip, shopping, tasks around the home. These are much more simple items to track that don't need the full complexity of something like Trello.

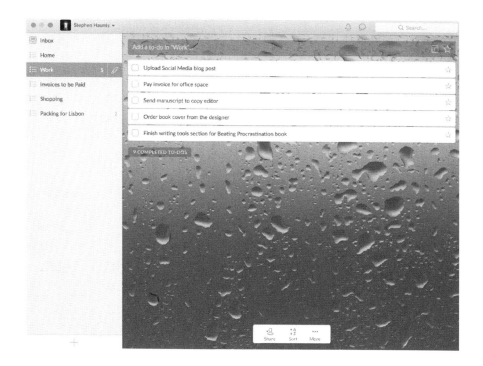

Once you have put items into a list in Wunderlist, you can open them up and set due dates, reminders, sub-tasks and add notes. You can run Wunderlist in a browser, as a native client for Windows, Mac, or iOS and Android phones and tablets. Like Trello, Wunderlist is free to use, but you can pay an upgrade fee to give you extras like assigning To-Do items to people, unlimited subtasks, and custom backgrounds.

Wunderlist isn't the only To-Do task application out there though. This is just my personal preference. There are other applications such as Todoist, and GoodTask to name a few, the specific tool isn't as important, but it's what the tool can do for you that is important.

iThoughtsX

The last tool or category of tools for planning that I want to
look at is mind mapping tools. In particular, the software
package I use is called iThoughtsX (available from
www.toketaware.com), but there are many different software
packages you can use across, Windows, MacOS, or mobile
platforms. iThoughtsX itself runs on MacOS, Windows and
iOS devices. What mind mapping tools allow you to do is get
your thoughts down on the screen quickly, and link those
thoughts together, annotate them with notes, add images, etc.
If you are trying to plan a new product or project and think up
ideas, then these types of tools are ideal for hierarchically
structuring your thoughts.

Whenever I design a new product or book, I always start by
thrashing around with ideas in iThoughtsX first.

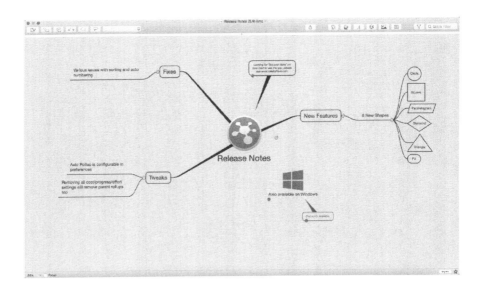

I have been using mind maps for many years, and I love the immediateness of them. Even if I don't have a computer handy, I will draw mind maps on a whiteboard. Here are some benefits of mind mapping.

Flexibility: Mind maps are very flexible in that you can use them for any purpose. It doesn't matter what the subject is or the purpose, mind maps are a straightforward way to document ideas quickly. Even when I was a student, I used mind maps as a way to revise complex subject. My revision notes were all mind maps, and I could augment the nodes on the mind map with notes in the mind mapping application for more detail.

Easy to Create: Mind maps are straightforward to create. All you need is an initial seed of an idea to get started. Then you just need a paper and pen, or a mind mapping application like iThoughtsX. You don't even need to write much as mind maps tend to work with much shorter words or phrases.

Clear and Visual: The primary focus of a mind map is its topic or subject. This always appears in the center of the mind map. Then extending from the central topic are different layers of nodes which can then drill down into that subtopic. This makes mind maps very easy to read and visually very clear. If you need to express ideas to other people instead of trying to explain it to them verbally, then show them the mind map instead and then use that as the basis of your explanation.

Fun and Creative: Most of all, mind mapping is fun to do and very creative. If I ever face a very complicated or scary set of tasks, I always use mind maps as a way to break down those tasks visually to enable me to understand the problem I am trying to grapple with more thoroughly.

Those are the tools I use to help me with the planning of either my time or tasks. The act of searching for tools can itself be a form of procrastination, so I hope that my suggestions prove to be useful to you. Let's now take a look at some tools that I use to help me focus when I am working on my tasks.

Focusing Tools

In our modern life, there are many distractions that all compete for our time; this time that is very precious, so any assistance using our daily tools will be of great benefit. The following software tools are all tool that I use myself every day to help me with my work. In fact, I am using them to write this very chapter that you are reading now. Let's take a closer look.

Noizio

The first tool I recommend is an application called Noizio which is available from noiz.io. I run this on MacOS, but it is also available on iOS. This app lets you mix different noise elements to create noise mixes. For example, you could combine rain, wind, and water to form a noisescape. This is ideal for you when you are in a noisy environment like a coffee shop or airport, and you want to drown out the world around you for you to focus. I use this application all the time in combination with a decent set of noise-canceling headphones. This allows me to drown out the rest of the world altogether.

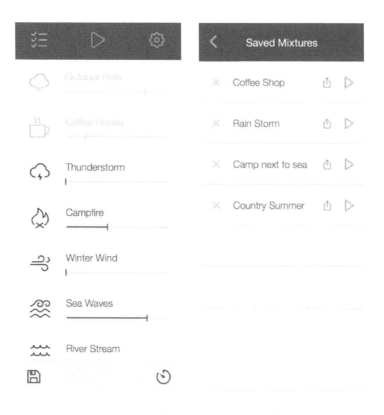

An application like Noizio is ideal If you want to focus but are not in the mood to listen to music. The soundscapes you create are very relaxing and help you concentrate.

If you don't use an Apple Mac or own an iPhone, then there is a great alternative called Noisli, which is available from www.noisli.com. This version has pretty much, the same feature set as Noizio, but it also runs in a browser and is available for Android too. It doesn't matter which one you use as they both let you achieve the same goal. When I want to concentrate I either use one of these apps (I use Noizio) or I listen to film scores as they don't tend to have vocals. I find it hard to concentrate on my work with music that has vocals a lot of the time, so instrumental music like film scores works well for me, or I use one of these noise generator apps.

Coffitivity

There is another form of noise app that I like to use called Coffitivity which is available from coffitivity.com. I have included this separately as it is a little different to Noizio and Noisli in that it only plays ambiance of coffee shops. You most likely have the same question in your head that I did when I first heard of this. "If this is just coffee shop noises and you are working in a coffee shop, why not just take your headphones off and listen to the real coffee shop noises?"

This is a fair question, but in all the coffee shops I work in, they always seem to be playing music over a PA system, and this music tends to be very bad. Of course, music is very subjective, but I can't ever see a coffee shop playing my style of music. This was even more annoying in December as all the coffee shops seem to be playing Christmas music which gets very irritating very quickly.

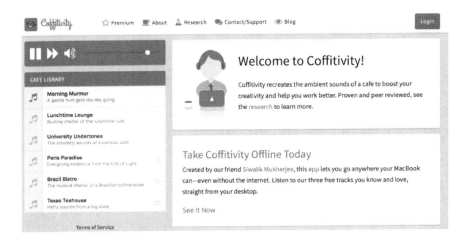

What is very interesting is that on the Coffitivity site there is a link to some peer-reviewed research about the effects of noise on concentration. You can read more about this research from coffitivity.com/research. But this is what their description states on their site.

"Everybody says their product is proven by research, right? Well...ours actually is.

According to a peer-reviewed study out of the University of Chicago, "A moderate level of ambient noise is conducive to creative cognition." In a nutshell, this means being a tiny bit distracted helps you be more creative. This is why those AHA moments happen when we're brushing our teeth, taking a shower, or mowing the lawn! If we're not focused too much on a task at hand, we come up with awesome stuff. In the coffee shop, the chatter and clatter actually distract us a tiny bit and allows our creative juices to start flowing. It sounds crazy, but it works!"

It's quite fascinating, and I highly recommend you going to read the scientific paper that is available from their site.

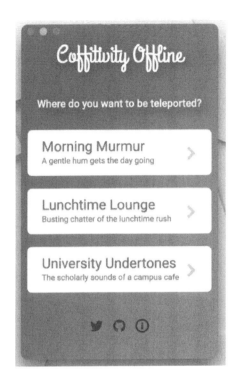

As well as working from the browser, Coffitivity is also available as a MacOS application and an iOS app.

Be Focused Pro

The next application I want to talk about is called Be Focused Pro which is available from xwavesoft.com/be-focused-pro-for-iphone-ipad-mac-os-x.html. Be Focused Pro is a timer application that you can set fixed intervals that you work. For example, you might set the timer for 25 minutes, and in that 25 minutes, you focus entirely on getting work done. In that time interval, you work as hard as you can for 25 minutes with no distractions. This means to close the browser and email, put your phone on silent and only do work.

Then when you have completed that interval, you take a break, say 5 or 10 minutes. Then you do it all again.

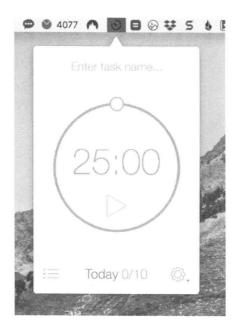

The idea is that by really concentrating for 25 minutes at a time with no distractions, you will get more work overall. This technique is called the Pomodoro technique. Be Focused Pro is available for MacOS and iOS, but you don't necessarily have to use this tool. There are many tools out there that do the same thing, or you can just set a 25-minute timer on your phone or a site like tomato-timer.com. The tool itself is not important; what is important is the mental conditioning of working in 25-minutes intervals. You don't have to do 25-

minutes, but this is a common interval to use. Here is a typical Pomodoro process.

1. Decide what task or tasks you wish to achieve.
2. Start the timer, (typically 25 minutes).
3. Work on the task with all distractions removed.
4. At the end of the interval take a 5-minute break then repeat from step 2.
5. After you have done 4 intervals (or Pomodoro's as they are referred too), take a longer break of 15 – 30 minutes.

Focus

The final tool I want to discuss is called Focus from heyfocus.com. Sometimes just setting a 25-minute Pomodoro timer is not sufficient for you to concentrate and focus. It is very common for the lure of social media and other websites to distract us. It is all too easy just to load up Facebook to see what is happening, especially if we see a notification come through.

If this is something that you are likely to do, and I have fallen into that camp, then you need some additional help. The tool I use is called Focus. What this does, it lets you block individual websites for a specified amount of time, like the 25-minute interval you are supposed to be working on. If you try and access one of those sites, you get a nice inspirational quote appear instead.

It could also be tempting just to turn focus off though if you are determined to look at Facebook or Twitter. If that's the case, then you can enable what they call, hardcore mode. This means you cannot access the applications preferences mode or disable the time. So, once you have started the timer, it will keep blocking those sites until the time finishes. This is invaluable when you have to get work done, and you know you are prone to go off surfing the web.

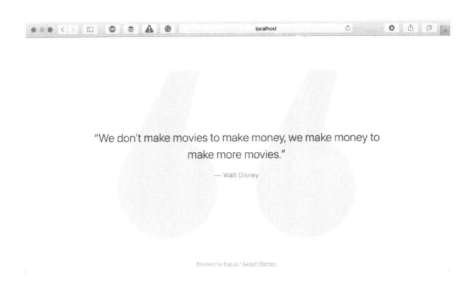

The list of sites is also customizable, so if there are sites you are likely to use that they haven't got on the default list, you can quickly add them. Focus is MacOS only; if you use Windows, then you can also look at FocusMe which is available from <u>focusme.com</u>. It is available for Windows and MacOS. FocusMe will also let you block applications from running too.

Again, the actual tool itself is not important; it's what the tool does for you that matters most in that it helps remove distractions that will stop you working.

Those are all the tools I wanted to cover. I have been trying different tools for many years, and these are the tools that I have settled with and used most days to help me with my planning and concentration. It is important to be careful with selecting tools as the process of trying tools can itself become a distraction and before you know it an entire day has disappeared without you getting your real work done.

Conclusion

Beating procrastination is no easy feat, especially if you have been doing it your entire adult life. However, with the help of the tips and tricks discussed in the chapters of this book, you should be able to do just that.

The next step is to create your personalized plan on how to go about this. First, you will need to choose the goal that you want to achieve. When you get rid of procrastination and have improved your ability to focus, you will be able to put more time and energy into your personal goals. You will be able to compete even with the best performing people in your workplace.

You want to fill your entire day with habits that lead to the completion of the goals you have set. To do this, you will need to choose carefully the tasks that you include on your to-do list. The idea is to eliminate tasks that will prevent or slow down your progress in reaching your goal.

Be aware of your thoughts and their effects on your behavior. In particular, you should become aware when thoughts and patterns of procrastination start creeping into your daily routine. You want to nip these habits in the bud. You can do this by using the tips in this book on how to get rid of procrastination.

Keep track of your fears and how you respond to them. In this book, we learned that many of these fears tend to have no immediate threat to our well-being. Because of this, the logical response to them is to face them. In the beginning, you will need to convince yourself to face these fears continually. With continued practice, you will be able to create a habit of beating these fears.

You will need to keep your mind focused on your goal and aimed to give 100% of your effort to it. The more you think actively about your goals, the better your chances are of beating your procrastination habit. Practice your ability to focus regularly and aim to keep your mind relaxed and ready to work.

Thank you for taking the time to read this book. I hope that it helped you understand your procrastination habits and find ways to get rid of it. Good luck!

Thank you for purchasing, A Gentle Introduction to Beating Procrastination and Getting Focused. If you liked this book, I would be very grateful for you leaving a review on Amazon. I read all reviews and will try to address any constructive feedback with updates to the book. You can review the book in your country at the following links, or from your local Amazon website.

Amazon.com
Amazon.co.uk
Amazon.de
Amazon.fr

If you enjoyed this book, you might like other books I have in the "Gentle Introduction To" series. I have written these short guides to focus on specific niches and make them brief enough to read in a short space of time, but also detailed enough that they offer a lot of value.

If you wish to see what other high-value books I have in this series, then please visit my web page at the following link.

Gentle Introduction To Book Series

Printed in Great Britain
by Amazon